A Gift of Peace and Purpose

A Survivor's Journey

Jeremy Wright

A Gift of Peace and Purpose: A Survivor's Journey
© 2020 by Jeremy Wright

ISBN (Print): 978-1-09831-943-4
ISBN (eBook): 978-1-09831-944-1

Special tribute to those who have lost their lives to cancer and suicide, those who struggle with mental illnesses and veterans. Some of the proceeds of this book will go towards cancer research, mental health awareness and suicide awareness.

Dear Me,

After a two-year journey of pressing through to the other side of the lessons that you were meant to learn in order to be where you are, you made it and it's time to get to work. Although life and learning doesn't stop here, you now have an understanding of what it is to truly be alive, to be at peace and to be in total alignment with the reason you are alive. Your "mistakes", the people you encountered, the circumstances you were in were all a part of the plan that was laid for you. This plan was designed to help your soul accomplish things that it needs to accomplish in this life time and as you submit to the process of the plan unfolding, your life blesses you abundantly in ways that you can never fathom. Your process forced you to disconnect from everything that you identified yourself with externally and helped you understand the importance of and how to identify with everything internally, as this is the source of everything and what connects you to everything and everyone. You cannot identify with things that parish like possessions. A sign of when you are not in submission to your process is if your life feels choppy or if you feel like you are resisting. Submitting to your process feels like you are dancing effortlessly to music instead of being off beat, floating with the current of calm waters instead of trying to swim against the current, or demonstrating mastery of a form of martial arts instead of fighting with no cadence. A part of the process that you struggled with at first was releasing control of how and when things happen because it is scary, especially after operating with the pressure of "what's next?" your entire lifetime. The only way the universe can bring things together in a way you will never be able to fathom is through releasing control. The plan that was laid out for you could not be successful without those who came before you, the environment that you were born in and the people and places that you have and will encounter at different phases of your life. Your soul will never endanger your life but will always allow circumstances and people to bring lessons that mold you for the sake of fulfilling its purpose and giving you choice. Never lose or give away your sense of self, peace or power, trust your process by releasing control of the how and when, and live life in a way that you will not look back with regret. Continue to love yourself unconditionally and know that everything that you need comes from within. Show people unconditional love and no judgement and one person at a time, you can change the world.

Quote: "I am not everything I possess; I possess everything that I am"

Speak It: "I am on a journey of peace and purpose, everything else is melting away."

Formula: Intention + Speak + Believe + Visualize + Emotion + Release + Action = What You Want

With all of the unconditional love from within,

The ME behind me

Dear Reader,

Thank you, from the bottom of my heart, for reading this book. My intention is to spark consciousness within you and format this book in a way that you can work through things at your own pace and with no judgement. In fact, I encourage you upfront to forgive yourself in advance so that you can tell yourself the entire truth no matter how difficult it may be to embrace. In recognizing that everyone learns differently, this book provides many ways to get to the same result in which you can also complete the separate self-guided journal. If you are open to my suggestion, read the entire book at your own pace and apply what makes sense to you. I assure you that you can overcome anything through mindfulness, optimism, patience, persistence, self-love and trust. It is my hope and prayer that at the end of this book you will have or at least know how to get peace in your life and you will be on or at least recognize the path to fulfilling your soul purpose in life. My goal is to capture not only that I survived what I thought was one of the worst things that could happen to me but also how my life experiences, people and circumstances, connected in a way that brought my entire life together so that you can do the same with yours without having to go through the headache of figuring it out like I did. This connectedness of life experiences positioned me to see how and why things were the way that they were. I hope and pray that you will feel encouraged to go on your own personal journey when you are ready and stay committed and optimistic as you will see in this book you can have peace and operate in your purpose. What's at stake if you do not go on this journey is what is perceived as the negative side of life; repeating the same lesson just with different people and places, being stuck in certain phases of your life, or never achieving your full potential. I feel the weight of life lifting off of you! I feel you taking your first breath of being alive! I feel your happiness and peace for you before it's already here! I see you in a place of peace and fulfillment while enjoying every moment of your life. I cannot wait to meet you and YOU.

With all of the unconditional love that I have,

Jeremy

The Golden Path

OUTCOME

After reading this book you will understand that you are starting on the path to peace and soul fulfillment. You will also know if you are ready to commit to the work necessary to make it happen. It is okay to acknowledge this is not a journey that you are able or willing to take right now. My hope, if you recognize you are not able to or willing to take this journey right now, is that you at some point come back to this journey and give it a try.

AUDIENCE

The Golden Path is for anyone who makes statements such as "Is there more to life than just paying bills", "I want more", "I am not fulfilled and I want to be", "When is my time?", "I feel empty", "I need peace", "I feel broken", "I want to leave a legacy", "I am happy but I want a deeper meaning to my life".

ABSTRACT

Everyone has their own journey they must go through. No one can force them self or another person to walk down a path that they are not ready for. It is up to each person to acknowledge, accept, commit to and walk down the path that is best for them. Unfortunately, sometimes our journeys start with a traumatic life experience but hopefully this book catches you before that happens. This journey requires that you leave the known for the unknown without concern of how and when things will happen. This journey guides you to finding peace and purpose from within so that you validate who you are at the core and no person or thing can shake you. In fact, ask yourself now without the name, the titles, the degrees, the house, the car or anything that is external to you, who are you? This journey starts with acknowledging that you want more out of life, starting down a path to a destination you may not be aware of, and ends with peace and the abundance of fulfilling your purpose in life, your destination.

QUOTE

"There is no right or wrong step in a journey; each step is still a step towards a destination."

SPEAK IT

"I am on the right path for me and I commit to doing the work."

FEEL IT

While being on the path you should feel excited, nervous or maybe even anxious that you are about to go on a journey that will change the trajectory of your life. Always remain optimistic about this journey as the way you feel and think will reflect in your circumstances. Optimism is important because on this journey you will want to break the commitment of going through until the end. If you are not optimistic, you will remain where you are and get the same outcome, if you are okay with that, all is well.

SEE IT

Imagine yourself with the ability to walk to any destination in the world across land and sea. Although there may be many ways to get to this destination, you make the decision of which way you will go, the pace you will walk, when you walk and when you stop. Consider your decisions in life, both conscious and unconscious, as steps on the way to your destination. Although we may perceive decisions or steps as good or bad, we should be aware that the outcome of that decision or step may make the journey to our destination easier, more difficult or take longer. The idea is to make conscious decisions or steps, so that we only make decisions or steps that are aligned with getting us to our destination in the best way possible. In spite of all of this, we are always on the path to our destination. As you commit to this journey, circumstances and people are there to condition you to be ready for your destination. When you ask questions like "Is there more to life?", life hears that you want to walk to a destination where there is more, although you may not know the where, how and how long. The distance from your conscious choice to pursue more in life to your destination, is the journey you must take on The Golden Path.

PRACTICE IT

You have to be very honest with yourself and say I don't care when, how, or how long; I am going to do better for myself. You have to be in a place of being relentless towards what you want. You have to sit down in that fact that you will uncover some ugly truths about yourself and your decisions yet not put on a pity party, sulk, or obsess about it. Forgive yourself and move forward. You have to be ready for people to walk away from you because their time in your life is over with or they don't understand where you are trying to go. You have to be honest with yourself about if you want to do the work that will come before you and if you want to dig deeper. You have to be in a place of knowing it is going to get tough temporarily but it will not always be this way. Assume the position, remain optimistic and don't give up! The end of this journey is worth what you will go through in order to get there, remain optimistic.

FORMULA

Acknowledgement of wanting more + Accepting that you will endure a lot + Commitment to doing the work + Doing the work consistently + Optimism about the outcome = The Golden Path (The journey we must all go on)

Activity

Journal the answer to the series of questions and reflect on how you feel about your honest answer. Decide if you are ready to go on this journey that may be difficult, painful or draining but temporary and very much worth it at the end.

Why am I taking this journey?

Knowing peace and purpose is at stake, are you willing to take this journey without concern of how long it will take and how things will come together?

Knowing that peace and purpose is at stake, are you willing to take ownership and responsibility for your actions both good, bad and ugly?

Knowing that peace and purpose is at stake, how will you handle losing your attachment to materialistic things, titles, jobs, money, people and anything else external to you?

Knowing that peace and purpose is at stake, how will you handle physically losing people and things?

Knowing that peace and purpose is at stake, how will you stay optimistic throughout this journey knowing that the work will be difficult and require you to be committed and consistent over an undefined amount of time?

Knowing that peace and purpose is at stake, how will you handle revealing who you truly are to the world?

Knowing that peace and purpose is at stake, are you okay with saying no to people and yes to yourself?

Hindsight

It's crazy how a few words can truly change your life. I remember that I received a base pay communication sheet from my manager that suggested my new salary for that year. I distinctly remember saying to myself, "nope, I don't know what I am going to do, but I am going to do something about it". In that moment I was not in the best environment at work, didn't trust too many people, and was desperately trying to get out. The communication within the organization was not good, there was no follow through and the ball kept getting dropped. I was exhausted with being one of the few people, who operated with integrity, who pushed and pushed to make things be the best that they could be. The sad part about it was that other people were reaping the benefits of my work, or so I thought. This moment when I said "no" was the start of The Golden Path for me. I was so sure that I was going to do everything in my power to change that situation. That conversation with myself in January of 2018 truly changed the trajectory of my life. In February of 2018 I went to Mardi Gras with my best friend and a mutual friend of ours. We had a good time for the most part and of course the food was amazing. The pivotal moment in this trip was when my friend wanted to go to have a tarot reading. As an open-minded person, I didn't think anything of it, it was an experience, although my upbringing would suggest that I do the opposite, I went along for the ride. Of course, we didn't know the popularity of this place and in fact it happened to be booked when we got there for the day. I don't know what it was but something within me said by the time we get ready to leave someone would call and cancel their booking and my best friend would be able to get her reading done. Before you know it, right before we walked out the door it happened, someone called and canceled and she was able to get a reading. I spent the next half hour with the mutual friend that we had looking at different crystals and gems secretly wishing I could be next for the reading but it wasn't my time. My best friend was more than convinced about the things that were being said as these were things only she knew personally that no one could look up on social media anywhere so I felt that it was real. After the trip I said that I would call and have a tarot reading over the phone as I wanted to experience it myself. In March of 2018 right before the call happened, a dear friend of mine suggested that I watch The Secret on Netflix. I watched it with an open mind as I unconsciously was searching for answers. I was truly bought into it from the moment I watched as it aligned with my upbringing of name it, claim it, it's yours for the asking, as the Clark Sisters sang. This however got put on hold after a very eye-opening reading. Everything that I knew was confirmed and some things that I wouldn't understand until later. The one thing that I took away from that reading was that there was something big that was going to happen, not necessarily a good thing, that would wipe my plate clean. I didn't keep that so close to me that I would get paranoid and it's a good thing because what I experienced next, literally broke me into pieces. March 31, 2018 at 11am I got the worst call of my life, my aunt passed away unexpectedly. I was on the couch watching YouTube videos with my best friend who I went to Margi Gras with. I didn't comprehend what happened but I knew that I was hurt deeply. I made a three-hour trip into a little over two hours. This was very hard for me to comprehend what was going on. I didn't connect that speaking what I did at the beginning of the year would bring this on me. I felt like I was broken into millions of pieces and the inside of me, whatever it may have been, was emptied. There were plenty of nights that I didn't sleep, to the point where I had to be prescribed medicine in order to get more than an hour of sleep. I truly felt abandoned, hurt, in rage and everything that I possibly could feel negative because of what happened. My aunt was so special to me as she taught me so many things about life. Having such a small family meant that any loss was a huge impact. A part of my foundation was truly ripped from under me and I had no motivation to do anything. In trying to understand what she was going through I decided to start reading her journals and her books. I had to do anything that I could to bring ease to my broken heart. In her readings what I took away was that in order for me to get through what I was going through, I had to make space for God to come in and heal me. In hindsight I realized that although my aunt's passing was not my fault, nor was it anyone's fault, it was a necessary life experience in order for me to wake up. One day as I was going through her pictures, every emotion that I could experience went raging through my body. All of the pint up emotion of everything that I had bottled up over the past 28 years ripped out of me at once. Everything from being molested at a young age, to being teased as a child because of my complexion and my mannerisms, to having two pistols pulled out and pointed in my face by a family member as I tried to come out to them, to having suicidal thoughts, to being in an abusive relationship where I almost died and tried to commit suicide several times, to experiencing the loss of my little brother to suicide who I blamed myself for and now this. For this to happen to me on top of all of this was unreal. I ran into my mom's bathroom and slammed the door and began punching the wall until there was no wall to punch. I felt myself slipping into a really deep black hole as if there was nothing that I would be able to do to come out of it if I kept going down. This hole felt like a void with nothing in it and was unwilling to let go of me until something within me said "Stop, or you will never be able to come back". My mom ran in the bathroom and hugged me with all of her strength as any mom would do. Something from within me saved my life. As the days went by, I continued to read my aunt's books and journals and started to watch YouTube videos on how to overcome depression. The psychiatrist that I was seeing was no help as he wasn't bought into me being healthy, it came across as him really wanting me to just get over it and take the medicine that he prescribed me for sleeping. I was thankful for my therapist who I had built a strong relationship with as she was an advocate for my well-being. She and I talked through so many things and I shared some of the things that my aunt was reading as well as some of the things that she wrote about me. In effort to try and pull myself together since my Psychiatrist wasn't helping, I went back to YouTube to see who else had gone through the same thing and was successful with living a healthy life. I came across a video of Eckart Tolle, describing his near-death experience and it resonated with me. I realized that what told me "no" was not something in me, it was me. At this point I started to recognize that the me that I had known all this time was not truly me but it was the human expression of who I was. This truly changed my life in a way that I will always be grateful. As I became obsessed with YouTube videos of Oprah and various guest talking about the soul, I began to be able to identify myself at a deeper level. One day, I began looking in the mirror, for the first time ever I was aware that I was looking at myself in the mirror. I began to cry as I knew that this was the awakening of my higher self. I grew more curious about being in the place of consciousness and was relentless in getting all that I could. I was more than committed to doing whatever was necessary for me to be all that I could be. For me, when this journey started, I did not know that I was going to go through everything that I would go through. In fact, I didn't imagine anything of that magnitude being possible to happen to me. What goes out into the universe does not come back as itself but whatever it is comes back with the same intention and strength that it went out with. If things did come back as the same thing, life wouldn't be life, in fact I am certain that what you speak comes back to you in the form of circumstances and people tied with a lesson to grant you access to what was spoken if you learn and apply the lesson. If not, you will end up in a life cycle of life experiences with the same lesson just different people and places. Although everyone will not have traumatic life experiences like mine that will cause them to ask those deep questions, for me it was necessary because I ignored signs from earlier in my life to wake up. Life was always trying to nudge me to wake up and it took large traumatic events in order for me to finally get the message. Don't let this be you, always do your best to listen to life as it will force you to get the message one way or another. I know that my awakening was necessary for me to give back to the world. It was important that I experienced this so that I could help others live a life that is fulling and to the best of their capabilities. Had I not committed to doing the work, there would have been more life experiences that may have taken me out completely. I never understood, while I was going through, why it happened to me but in making space for God to heal me I remained optimistic about the potential outcome. I know through experience, in spite of the pain of losing someone so close to me and all of the major life experiences that I endured, it is possible to achieve peace.

The Secret Garden

OUTCOME

After reading this book you will be able to identify your own secret garden, recognize the comfort of your secret garden, and be able to mentally stay in your secret garden which helps you to make decisions or steps on The Golden Path.

AUDIENCE

This is for anyone who makes statements such as "I have too many thoughts in my head going on at once", "My mind keeps racing and I don't know how to stop it", "I am cluttered", "I cannot focus on doing the work I need to do", "I feel stuck, I am willing to work but I don't know how to get unstuck", "I don't like where I am in life and I want to change it", "I am ready for change but don't know where to start", "I'm trying to change but people are not accepting that I am trying to change".

ABSTRACT

Once you acknowledge, accept, commit and are ready to walk down The Golden Path in an optimistic mind frame, you have to be in a place mentally that allows you to do the work. This mental place, The Secret Garden, is where you escape so that nothing and no one can disturb you. Having a place of serenity allows you the space to reflect and grow to ensure you are making the right decisions or steps on The Golden Path.

QUOTE

"Any action from me before I think is a sacrifice of my peace; nothing is worth my peace."

SPEAK IT

"I am in a place of reflection, growth, love, peace, and protection. These things are invaluable to me."

FEEL IT

While being in your secret garden it may start off uncomfortable, lonely, like you are being selfish, secluded, and distant but in the end, it will be peaceful and quiet within you. As you get comfortable with The Secret Garden you may start to notice how quickly people respond without thinking and start to get annoyed and you may start to notice that people are walking around as an empty shell in survival mode. Your secret garden will always be a place within yourself that creates ease and peace. It feels still, as if you could be in a stadium of 100,000 people yelling and screaming and still be at peace. As you become fully present you will experience that there is no internal noise in your secret garden.

SEE IT

Can you imagine the most beautiful destination in the world that you have an emotional tie to? If someone wanted to destroy that destination, how would you feel and what would you do to protect it? Imagine the most impassable barrier that you can think of in order to protect this beautiful destination so that it will not be destroyed. In the same way that you would protect this beautiful destination, you must guard yourself as you enter in The Secret Garden. This secret garden is a place of peace, it is where you go to ask and receive the answers to the questions of your heart. When you are committed to The Golden Path, there has to be a place of peace that allows you the space to reflect on your decisions without judgement and without concern of what people will do or say. The beauty of this destination is that it goes with you everywhere you go so that you can go there when you want to. The impassable barrier is your instinct and feeling. When someone or something violates that barrier, you must become fully present, if you are not already, and make conscious choices to your benefit. Do not act out of any emotion other than inner peace. As you get better with going to this place mentally you will recognize that you have created space between what may have happened to you and your reaction, this is the key to making decisions or steps while on The Golden Path. Welcome to your mental place of peace, The Secret Garden.

PRACTICE IT

Commit to doing grounding exercises and meditation as consistently and frequently as you possibly can. Perfect practice of grounding exercises and meditation makes perfect. You must dedicate as much time to this routine as possible as this helps you become present. Eventually, this practice of being present will "slow down time" as you are not focused on the past nor future but what is going on in this very moment. As you continue to practice this you will start to notice your mind get quiet and also the detail of everything around you. This clarity allows your higher sense of self to be the pilot of your actions and not your personality.

FORMULA

Present anchors + Focus on present anchors + No pressure to be present + Perfect Practice = The Secret Garden (The space to think about your decisions or steps and a quiet mind)

ACTIVITY

Journal your experience about grounding exercises and meditation. Light some candles or incense, turn on soft music, grab something in your hand, close your eyes and use your senses to hone in on what you smell, hear and feel. Please do not get frustrated if it doesn't work on the first try as "perfect practice makes perfect." You must be relentless in practicing this as this is very key to everything else. To help with identifying your soul versus your personality put on a costume of some sort and stand in the mirror. You are aware that you are not the costume that you are wearing, you are you inside of the costume. With this same concept your body is the costume and you are the awareness that you are in a costume. You could also watch the ancient one in Dr. Strange punch the awareness of Dr. Strange out of the physical Dr. Strange. Routinely look in the mirror and say to yourself, "I am not the me that I am looking at, I am not my body that I can touch, I am the awareness of me that I am looking at and can touch." Imagine that the awareness of you can take a "step back" and watch your body standing as if you are having an out of body experience. One day you will go outside and recognize the beauty of the world and breathe your first breath of being alive.

HINDSIGHT

The awakening of myself was the best thing that had ever happened to me. This awakening was like walking around in need of glasses and then finding the right pair for me so that I could see with great clarity. It was like I was walking through a huge forest but all of a sudden, I noticed the pattern of each tree trunk. I used my senses to focus on things in the present, such as sitting on the porch every night, listening to the wind as it whipped by my porch or moved the leaves on the trees back and forth against each other or the crickets chirp on the ground, feeling the warmth of the candles that I would burn, feeling the coldness of the glass of wine that I would drink out of, and watching the stars and the moon. All of this helped to bring me fully present to the moment that I had to were nothing else was a concern. Although I didn't realize it at the time, this was a form of meditation for me. It allowed me to regulate my senses, especially of self, to the point that I had no internal noise and thus peace within myself. I had never realized the true beauty of the earth until I started to hone in on being present at my will. The trees had never been so green before, there were buildings that I started to notice that I had never seen before, and I never realized how big Walmart was until I started to look up to see the rafters. To me, being on the porch at night was my secret garden. It was a place that no one knew existed except me as I was able to escape all of the noise in my life. By this time, it was summer of 2018 and I had gone back to work after being off for a few months to gather myself. It was the same environment that was there when I left with the exception of me being the one who changed. I knew that I gave off the vibe of not wanting to be there but this new found ability to have peace within myself while being in chaos was something that I had to learn. I was so thankful that a dear friend of mine had taken over my responsibilities while I was out of office so that I could transition back into my role. I knew that she would cover me as she knew I wasn't mentally at work. In fact, whenever I said "I'm on the porch", that was my way of telling her that I was imagining myself at home at night looking up at the stars and the moon and had no concern of the noise and chaos that was going on around me. This worked very well as I began to adjust my attitude to be more positive than it had been. I continued my nightly routine of sitting outside at night and my obsession of Oprah videos on YouTube. I picked up where I left off with The Secret and as I continued to share my experiences of being on the porch and The Secret with my dear friend, she told me that Jim Carey wrote a check to himself and was later able to cash it due to him following his passion of acting and I was convinced that I would be able to do the same thing but because of whatever my passion was. In fact, I would take it a step further and wrote myself a check for $450 million and created an entire vision board of things that I wanted to achieve, people that I wanted to meet, and anything that came to mind such as philanthropy and helping certain causes. At this time, I wasn't connecting what I said in January of that year to what was going on but it was sure to happen. I was faithful to my nightly routine, faithful to my vision board and faithful to the things that I was learning from what I now deemed as YouTube University. As I continued my routines, I started to notice patterns of things happening to me. I was "on the porch" mentally more and more which created space for me to be very aware of what was going on around me. When people would say or do certain things I would go "on the porch" to try and figure out what I was supposed to take from that. I started to realize that my stress of being in a noisy and chaotic environment went away because I was no longer taking on people and what they said or did but I was going inward to reflect on what this person or circumstance was here to teach me to be a better me. One day

I heard a young lady vent about a customer by saying, "you have all of this money and you are being cheap." As a member of management, this caught my ear and in fact my initial reaction was that statement was totally out of line. Since I had developed a habit of creating space before I react, I couldn't help but think why did I catch onto that of all things that people are saying around me. That same sense of self that told me to "stop" in the midst of my breakdown as I was grieving my aunt said you will be a millionaire. I looked down at the time and it was 2:52pm on a Saturday. This was weird to me until I remembered that I wrote myself a check for $450 million and put it on my vision board next to the jackpot or lottery. I also remembered in this moment from YouTube University that I had watched a video from Oprah talking about the whispers of life and how life allows certain things to get your attention. Although I didn't take it literally, in that moment, that I would be a millionaire I was on high alert for something I just didn't know what. What was crazy about this was that after that moment, for weeks and weeks, I started seeing the number 252 all over the place and decided to look it up. It meant that I was in a place that I was not happy and that my guardian angels were trying to get my attention. It meant that I was oppressed and not able to do things that came naturally to me. It also meant that eventually things would make sense and all of my worries especially finances would go away. What was even more crazy was that the meaning of this number was exactly what was said when I had my tarot reading back in March of that year. I started to connect things together and realized that this had to be a sign that a huge breakthrough was coming my way. As I continued my routines and 252 continued to show up one day someone brought to my attention that the lottery was getting bigger and bigger. During this time, I remember watching the news and advisors were giving their suggestions on what to do with it and the math after taxes had broken down to no other number than $450 million. Of course, at that point, I played the lottery as I would've loved to have won that amount of money as a "quick fix" to all of my perceived problems. One day, I woke up and what do you know? The winning ticket had been sold in the city I was living in and I went completely numb. What I knew in that moment was that my intention in winning the lottery was not to live this lavish lifestyle but to live comfortably on a budget and do a lot of philanthropy work like I had put on my vision board. As the day went on, I realized that I wasn't the winner and I was ok with that. I knew that my routine had impact on the way that my life could turn out and that was a lottery that I was thankful that I had won. This consistent pattern of going inward, to a place that I could be at peace, looking to take away from people and circumstances what was meant for me to take away, to make the right decisions I needed to make in order to bring myself out of where I was is exactly what this part of my life was meant for. Had I not gone through an awakening I wouldn't have been able to piece things together as I did. I didn't need millions of dollars to be at peace or be happy, I was already at peace and happy because of the routine that I had of being present and knowing that my journey had a purpose. There are so many people in the world who have financial wealth beyond comprehension who are empty and unfulfilled that would give everything they have away just for peace and purpose. It's sad to see someone filling a void with external things to never truly be satisfied, this is why you must accept that everything you need is already inside of you and anything external cannot and will not bring you peace or fulfilment. My tone at work started to change and I started to be my optimistic happy self again. I realize now that this environment was meant to teach me something so that I could move on with no attachment from my circumstance at that point of my life while applying the lessons that I had learned. Your circumstance will not allow you to be comfortable because you will get complacent and not push to learn what you need in order to move forward. If you are always reaching but falling short, constantly running into unwelcoming situations or just seem not to be able to get comfortable this maybe a sign to go inward to your secret garden to trust the process that you maybe in without knowing it. Trusting my routine, I worked to really manifest something that I knew that I wanted, a different job that would allow me to explore myself even more. I wrote what I wanted on a piece of paper and stuck it in my badge holder and began the interview process for multiple jobs. I heard no more times than I cared to hear but I knew that there was a reason for this to happen. Going back "on the porch" I reasoned with myself that there was something good enough for me and that these nos are happening for a reason. Eventually, I got the phone call, the offer I had been waiting for and I said yes. I moved my life of 29 years all the way across the US. This environment was totally different than what I was used to. I was fully prepared to do the work necessary for me to get where I needed to be personally and professionally. I hit the ground running and was fairly successful and effective at my new job within a short time frame. I still managed to keep my routines although not as consistent as I had a lot going on with a new environment, new job, and I was getting my MBA. I started to modify my routine to my new house and instead of sitting outside at night, I started to do meditation and yoga while listening to music. My routine was so effective that I started to recognize even more patterns, specifically with people. There were common themes that I noticed had followed me that I didn't address before, this solidifies the importance of having a place to go inward to identify, learn and apply the lessons so you don't have to repeat them. It was imperative that I addressed these lessons so that I could continue to grow. I noticed that a lesson not learned turns into a life cycle which to me meant that I would cycle through the same lesson disguised as a circumstance with different people in a different place. As I continued my routine and started to journal these lessons that I was able to identify in interacting with certain people and circumstances, I realized that they all started to sync together in a way that I never would have thought. From this moment I started to see a web of life events that were designed to teach me things and to wake me up. What I didn't realize as I was walking around sleep walking in life was that the circumstances for me got more traumatic as I went on in life ignoring what I was meant to take from them. I recognized that people started to have common behaviors and in a weird way almost started looking like each other. Being human I still struggled with not getting caught up in the moment but taking a step back to say, although this is not the ideal circumstance to be in there is something that this is meant to teach me. Recognizing this made things speed up for me in terms of getting confirmation that the journey that I was on was The Golden Path to my peace and purpose.

The Seed of You

OUTCOME

After reading this book you will be able to identify that you are in a process and most importantly have faith in the process as you release concern of the how and when. You may begin to recognize the different parts of your process by seeing how different circumstances and people bring various lessons to help mold you according to what's necessary for your plan. You will start to peel off layers that have wrapped around you about who you should and should not be, what you should and should not do, or how things should or should not unfold. You will further explore the importance of constantly being in The Secret Garden to reflect on your decisions or steps on The Golden Path.

AUDIENCE

This is for anyone who makes statements like "I want to get better but I don't want it to take forever", "Change is difficult and uncomfortable", "I am trying to change but I don't see any progress", "I am trying to make things work but I cannot figure out how to do it", "why do I keep going through the same thing", "this always happens".

ABSTRACT

Once you know the comfort of your secret garden you must be optimistic that the path you are own has a purpose. You must accept that the destination will come and will be worth the path you must take without concern of the how and when. You must get extremely comfortable with not being in control of the how and when of your process. People and circumstance are a part of your process and the lessons that are tied to them will show up in a different form should you choose not to learn it. Remember that perfect practice of going to The Secret Garden and addressing your response to people and circumstances makes perfect. You are addressing and changing behaviors that has been in place over a long period of time and this requires you to make going to The Secret Garden a habit.

QUOTE

"I cannot be what I am not, I can only be what I am, I am what I am."

SPEAK IT

"I am thankful for and trust the process that I am on without concern of the how and when things will manifest."

FEEL IT

While in the process you will feel out of control, you will need to submit to the process and feel like you are floating in a body of water going with the current instead of trying to walk against the current. Your gut will feel unease at first but eventually you will be comfortable with being uncomfortable. This is why you must know the comfort of your secret garden as you will feel unease with being out of control. You will want to try and act on something without thinking of how whatever you are going through is important to the path that you are on. Remember that circumstances and people are there to condition you for your destination. Continually go into The Secret Garden when you feel unease to create space between what is happening to you and your decisions to help you get through the process.

See It

Can you imagine the most beautiful apple that you have ever seen? Imagine that you have cut the apple in half in order to eat it and you see the seeds within it. This seed that you are looking at inside of an apple, if planted, could become nothing other than an apple tree. It knows that it is an apple tree without concern of how and when it will become an apple tree. The moment the apple seed makes the decision or step, conscious or unconscious, to become an orange tree, the process of the apple tree does not stop but it will become more difficult or take longer. The apple seed has to sort through trying to become an orange tree and then continue down the path of becoming an apple tree. Trust the process of you, the seed, becoming what you need to be in order to be ready for your destination. Being aware that circumstances and people are a part of the process should cause you to be intentional about your decisions or steps as they will have an impact of how long the process will be. Go to The Secret Garden to reflect on why you are in certain circumstances and why certain people are in your life. Be aware that everyone is on a path of their own that you may cross but not necessarily The Golden Path. You being on The Golden Path may spark their desire to want more in life. You will have to go through a circumstance or have an experience with a person or people in order to be prepared for your destination. There is a constant theme that life is trying to bring to your attention but you must be in the mental space to take a step back in order to have space to ask questions, reflect and grow.

Practice It

Put the emergency brakes on whatever you thought your plan was. Stop trying to be in control. Stop trying to meet timelines. Stop trying to make plans other than the plan that was already laid for you. Stop trying to live up to other people's dream about your life. Just stop, just be you and just be. With your safety first, go to a pool and float, this is what being in flow is like and in contrast try to run in that same pool, this is what it is like to be out of flow. As you practice letting go in each moment of your life, go to The Secret Garden and ask "What am I to learn from this circumstance or this person?" Once you get in the habit of taking a step back, you will notice a pattern of things that link together and you will be able to spot a lesson in the making. Identify that this circumstance or person is trying to bring a lesson to you in order to make you ready for your destination, accept that it is inevitable and that you will repeat this lesson until you get it. Trying to be in control of the process or not learning the lesson will only bring different people in a different place with the same lesson tied to it. The faster you get this, the faster you will move through your process. Without The Secret Garden you would have no space to reflect and grow on what is happening and would be in constant control of trying to make things work thus, taking steps down a path that is not The Golden Path. The grounding exercises and meditation will help you be present so that you think before you react, that space allows you to analyze everything about your circumstance so that you make a decision for the best possible outcome. Look beyond the person and circumstance to see the lesson that they are and release control of and submit to the process so that you can move further down The Golden Path.

FORMULA

Give up control + Submit to the process + Identify the lesson + Accept the lesson + Learn the lesson + Apply the lesson = The Seed of You (The process of you being readied for your destination)

ACTIVITY

Journal your experience, daily, of planting a seed of anything and tend to it as needed with the right conditions until you see it be what it is supposed to be. Notice that regardless of how you feel during this process, the seed will be what the seed is. Trust your process, people and circumstances are necessary ingredients to you being what you will be. They are like soil, a flower pot, fertilizer, water and everything necessary to make the seed be what it will be. The seed could never grow without the necessary things it needs. This is a representation of how you must be, trust your process, people and circumstances help you grow into what you need to be in order to be what you will be.

HINDSIGHT

I would have never imagined that what I said in January of 2018 and what I put on my vision board would have went into what could be considered as the future to arrange people and circumstances in a way that I would be blown away. I continued my routine of meditating and yoga in addition to journaling in order to reflect on the people and circumstances in my life; this was now a habit that I had been doing for months now. My journaling allowed me to see that I truly can do or manifest anything that I wanted to if my intentions are right and I was willing to submit to the process that involves people and circumstances to prepare me for it. When things go out into the universe it will never come back in a way that you would expect as it would make life too easy. I appreciated this lottery winning of wisdom at such a young age as I knew the rest of my life would be much easier in knowing this. My journaling helped me connect how my words from January 2018 had impacted my life in such a way that in 2019, I would still be wrapping my head around things. What I also appreciated about this discovery at such as young age was that the labels, expectations and other chains that people, including myself, put on me started to go away to reveal my true nature that was aligned with my soul purpose. This meant that I was no longer putting value in what was projected on my life but putting value in what I understood to be the reason my soul existed. I took away what I was supposed to from those circumstances or people but not the weight of the circumstance or person itself, this is not easy to do. I realized that life events are about choices that we make and those choices are what ties our lives to each other's based on where we are individually in our lives for a bigger plan. It is difficult to swallow, hearing such a horrible thing to happen to a child such as molestation may be for the person who committed the act to trigger a series of life events to get them in check and maybe as that child grows up they learn to speak on what they experienced which sets so many people free and puts a spotlight on family or community issues that need to be addressed to break generational curses. For someone to experience such trauma as being bullied and picked on because of things that they cannot control, this may be necessary for this individual to find confidence to climb their way up a corporate ladder to be the CEO of a company or for those who did the bullying to realize when they see that CEO that they picked on that they were hurting because of something they were lacking in their childhood. For me to have two pistols pulled out and loaded in my face was necessary to severe a relationship that would have held me captive and may have been manipulative in a way that kept me chained enough to have some comfort in life but not ever experience true freedom which may have caused the person who did this to experience loneliness and to look past something to love a person for who they are. For me to have experienced a life-threatening relationship, attempted to commit suicide and experience life after having someone I loved committing suicide on two occasions I needed to be shaken so that I could wake up. The image that I tried to maintain as a result of being in the preacher's family, the mannerism that I tried to mask, and the hurt that I tried to hide; all of these layers and mask had to come off in order for my true potential to come forth. As I started to have these deeper revelations, it offended my soul to magnify something in a way that it was not meant to impact my life. Being "on the porch" allowed me to truly scale back my reaction towards people and circumstances so that I could see the lesson that it was. I could not give someone the ability to influence my life or give them power enough to change my mind, mood, or motivation especially when I recognized that they were nothing more than a lesson. In having a habit of bringing "the porch" with me everywhere that I went, it was so easy for me to see beyond a person or a circumstance for what it was at the surface. This made it easier for me to let go of trying to control things and simply let things unfold while being aware that there was a lesson not far behind, somewhat like playing double dutch and looking for when you should jump. I was always mindful of my posture in certain situations and truly mindful of what I said and what I did. My "porch" became my buffer and I would not let anything or anyone disturb the progress that I was making as it was my focus to move forward in my journey as quickly as possible. If I did allow someone to get under my skin, it didn't last long because I came back to asking "what is the lesson and is me not learning and applying the lesson worth a round two?" My journaling helped me to reflect on what I was doing that was effortless to me and what I often poured into people in order to make their situations better. The themes of people and circumstances always came back to the same point. This was when I truly realized that I had a gift of helping people be conscious of their decisions so that they could live a better life. There was such an ease about doing this that doing anything other than this violated the feeling of being "on the porch." In being aware of what came naturally to me and that the people and circumstances that crossed paths with me often had a lesson tied to them, I started to hone in on the skills that I needed to be more effective such as coaching skills, empathy, emotional intelligence, and project management. I had been coaching people for the past 6 years but coaching them to meet performance objectives that were set by the organization that I was working in at the time. This ability to be energized by helping people achieve life goals but vexed to manage their performance or anything not related to them getting better in life was a big red sign that my gift was right in front of me. This gift was right in front of me my entire life but because I was not conscious or awoken yet, I would never know to look down and pick up my gift to the world. Life was trying to get me to wake up all along but I was sleepwalking throughout life making decisions that were always going to get me to my destination but in a roundabout way. Now that I was no longer sleep walking, now that I had put on my glasses, now that I see the tree trunks on each tree in the forest, I started to trust my process and allow people and circumstances to teach me and not to define me, I was more at ease within myself. Realizing that people were walking around in life as an empty shell, not conscious of their choices, not thinking about the impact of their decisions was something that I was passionate about changing. Trusting my process to be whatever I would be had now brought me to knowing my purpose in life.

What are you Pouring?

OUTCOME

After reading this book you will know what your soul, the awareness of you, decided to fulfill in this journey of life. You will recognize your soul purpose and the feeling of operating in your purpose. Your gift, your soul purpose, can only be used effectively once you have gone through your process, The Seed of You.

AUDIENCE

This is for anyone who makes statements like "I don't know what my purpose in life is", "I don't know what I am good at", "Nobody will want to listen to what I have to say", "I want to make a difference", "I want to leave a legacy".

ABSTRACT

Once you have faith that the process is for your good, you have to realize that the process is preparing you to birth something. That something can be small or large to you but that something needs to come forth in order for the world to be a better place and for your soul to be at peace. Your soul's purpose, the gift you have, is a part of the outcome of the process that you must go through and have faith in. Your purpose is connected to the lessons that you learn.

QUOTE

"My gift is not for me; it is for the world. Without me and without my gift, the world could never be what it is meant to be."

SPEAK IT

"I am fulfilling my soul purpose and it feels amazing to know how I can contribute to helping the world be a better place."

FEEL IT

While you are figuring out your soul purpose you will feel curious, like you will be finding your footing, you may start to or have already connected the dots of why your process is what it is and at the end you should feel ease when you are using your gift, your soul purpose and the contrary when doing anything else.

SEE IT

Can you imagine receiving the gift that you have always wanted no matter the cost? This gift is so precious that you may have thought it was impossible or too far-fetched for you to ever have it in your possession. This gift means so much to you that if you received it, it would invoke many emotions. This gift feels so precious that you would protect it as much as you possibly could. In order for this gift to be so precious, that you thought it was impossible or too far-fetched for you to obtain, it means that you recognize the amount of resources it took to get this gift. You are born with a precious gift; it is the reason for your life. Your start does not define who you are, it was the necessary circumstance and group of people needed for you to be ready for your destination. This gift may be small or big to you but when you give it to the right person, they feel the same way you would feel as if you were to receive the gift that you have always wanted no matter the cost. The process of this gift coming into existence cannot be rushed as the impact or value of gift will not be the same. As you sit in The Secret Garden and plant The Seed of You, consider that this seed must grow until it is ready which means you and the lessons you were meant to learn have all aligned. At the right time, you will give your gift to the world, you now know exactly what you are pouring.

PRACTICE IT

Reflection on your circumstances and lessons is key, this is another reason why The Secret Garden is so important. Do you notice a pattern in each circumstance that you are in? Does the lesson of your circumstances connect to each other? When you piece everything together, how can you use this outcome to be of service to people? This outcome, your purpose, is the reason you have a beat in your heart. Without you the world is not able to be as bright as it could be. As you are of service to people with what you have discovered to be your purpose, people's lives change for the better. As you continue to pour your gift life will bless you as you bless other people.

FORMULA

Linking the lessons learned and circumstances together + Applying lessons learned + Being of service to people with your linked lessons learned and circumstances = What you are Pouring (Your gift to the world)

ACTIVITY

Journal common themes in your life; what do certain people that may irk you or need something from you have in common and reflect inward? Remember that as you go to The Secret Garden, there are lessons you are constantly looking for tied to people and circumstances as they make you ready for your destination. Do you need to stop leeching off people? Do you need to speak up more often? Do you get asked your expertise on something all of the time? What is tripping you up in each situation you encounter and is it the same thing every time? When you apply the lesson that you learned from the common circumstances, does your life suddenly have an ease about it?

Hindsight

Coaching people was like breathing air to me. It was a natural conversation that I would have with people that would get their eyes to open up. I set a boundary that it was never my responsibility to get them to execute on their new found understanding but simply to help them wake up in a sense to see the bigger picture. Time after time things continued to come together in a way that gave me great relief. I understood why life had me experience the things that I had experienced. Life was trying to get me to wake up so that I could truly fulfill the purpose of my soul. These huge life events were signs that were meant for me to wake up to my higher self. These life experiences, circumstances, and people were a part of my life in order for me to eventually come to this point of knowing exactly what I was supposed to do in life. As I continued my routine and journaling, I realized that not only was the past 6 years of me coaching aligned with my purpose in life but I was able to trace things from this point all the way back to my first job. I always had a job where I was helping people make decisions and living an easier life and I was good at it; I just wasn't aware of it. In addition to tracing things back to my first job, I was able to trace things back to my upbringing, who I was born to, the people who raised me, where I was born and when I was born. The totality of my environment, people and circumstances from the beginning were necessary for my life to be what it would be. At this point in my journey things were very natural to me in terms of interacting with people and being in various circumstances. I was not phased at some points because I knew that what I was going through was not about whatever it seemed to be on the surface, it was all about me learning something to be better at my life purpose. With that being said I am very thankful for the organization that I worked in that was noisy and chaotic, I am very thankful for the people whose paths that I have crossed which was confirmation and or necessary in order for me to be ready for my destination, I am thankful for the time that I was able to spend with my aunt for the 28 years we had together. In being able to help people become conscious of their decisions, I know that I in return will be rewarded so that I can keep doing what my life was destined for. Life will not put things in your way in that manner. When you are honoring the reason for your life it encourages you to keep pressing forward with random blessings popping up as somewhat of a reward for doing the right thing so that you only focus on your life purpose. It wouldn't make sense for life to not meet all of your needs if you are doing the right things as it would be counterproductive. For me I noticed that miracles of all sizes would happen such as my financial situation started to change for the better in ways that I couldn't explain, people who I never would have imagined started coming into my life were able to connect me with other people of influence that genuinely cared for my wellbeing and helped me to get to the right place at the right time beyond what I thought was possible, and I began to experience the reality of my vision board coming to life. It was almost like life was peeping over my shoulder and saying "Look at that, you finally get it! Here is a blessing, here is a blessing, and here is a blessing". In moving forward with this desire to want to help the world, I had to realize that I was still human and have to set boundaries for myself which included keeping my buffer of being "on the porch".

Capacity to Pour

OUTCOME

After reading this book you will know when and when not to pour your gift. You will also realize that people often do not have the capacity to pour into you. You cannot expect someone to pour something into you when they do not know what or have the ability to pour. You may have realized this when people started to disappear out of your life when you started going into The Secret Garden.

AUDIENCE

This is for anyone who makes statements like "People take advantage of me and I feel drained", "I am exhausted and want to help but I just don't have the energy", "I am giving to people but never receive anything back", "I am always coming to the rescue of others but I need a shoulder too".

ABSTRACT

Once you know your purpose in life, what you are pouring, you will want to share it with the world. It will feel good to operate in your purpose but you have to take care of yourself. Our intentions when pouring and the condition must be right in order to pour and be poured into.

QUOTE

"What I am pouring into will carry the intention and condition in which I pour. I pour when my intention and condition are right so that what I pour into can grow."

SPEAK IT

"I am in the right space to pour out and be poured into. When I am not, I choose me every time."

FEEL IT

When you are pouring your gift into people you feel amazing and can do it without a break. It feels like you are at ease, like you are alive and feel joyful. There is nothing that can stop you from pouring. You must always be in The Secret Garden in order to know when enough is enough. Going beyond enough is a quick way to end up risking your wellbeing.

SEE IT

Can you imagine your car running out of gas in the desert with a temperature of over 100 degrees, a dead cell-phone, and a 10-mile walk to the nearest town? Once you have arrived to the gas station you realize that the gas container cost twice as much as it normally would but, you are able to get enough gas in order to get you back to town so that you can fill up your gas tank all the way. As you are two miles into your 10-mile walk back you notice that there is a car up ahead that is pulled over. As you get closer to the car you notice that their gas tank is open only to come to the conclusion that they have run out of gas just like you have. Once you approach the car, you notice that it has a large family with an elderly parent and a new born baby in the car seat. If they ask you if you can spare some gas so that they can get to town, will you spare them gas knowing that you have only enough gas to get you back to town without giving any to someone else? You must know when you have the capacity to give and when you do not. If you give to the point of not having enough for yourself, you have crippled your ability to be of service to those who are in need and yourself. After you realize you know what you are pouring into the world as a gift, you must be in constant communication with yourself to know when it is right for you to pour and when it is not. The Secret Garden is the place for you to recognize your intention and the condition.

PRACTICE IT

Place a space between your circumstance and your reaction. Go into The Secret Garden to check your intentions and the condition of the situation to know if you should pour or not and also if you are ready to be poured into.

FORMULA

Being in The Secret Garden + Having the right intention + Conditions being right = Capacity to Pour

ACTIVITY

Journal more about what you are noticing when you are giving your gift. Balance giving your gift with self-care. Set boundaries based on feeling of ease and unease, remember this as the barrier to The Secret Garden. Trust your instinct and realize your process has led you this far. Reflect on how you can also pour your gift into someone but they may not be ready to receive it and also how people may not be able to pour into you if you are not ready to receive or they are not capable of doing so.

HINDSIGHT

At this point in my journey I am getting really good at this thing! I am in a constant state of "being on the porch" which acts as a buffer for me to act appropriately in every circumstance that I find myself in. I stay focused on operating in flow with my life purpose, as all of my needs are met and things effortlessly line up in a way that I would have never been able to piece it together. My gift was only used when I went "on the porch" and felt my intention and the condition was right; I saw positive changes in peoples' lives when they decided to apply what I coached them about. In the most politically correct way I would say "Thank you but no thank you" if I felt unease about a situation; I consistently applied a lesson of knowing and enforcing my boundaries which made life easier for me. Besides the traumatic life experiences that brought me to this moment, now that I am on the other side of things, everything else was and is so minor. What caused them to be major was my unconscious resistance to identifying, learning and applying the lesson tied to the circumstance or person as if I forgot to look or didn't care to see when the rope was coming for me to jump. My "No" from January 2018 was my beacon to life to say that I was ready for more in life. The passing of my Aunt was a way of wiping my plate and myself completely clean so that I could make space for the work that was needed. The awakening that I experienced was to make me aware of the circumstances that I was in so that I could make decisions that were to my benefit. The people that I encountered were either signs on the side of the road to be cautious and be ready to learn lessons so that I could apply what I learned and move forward or confirmation that everything was going to be alright. My awakening that created the space for me to do the work allowed me to step back and see the bigger picture of why things were the way that they were. My routine, that I practice daily, grounds me and keeps me still so that I can hear and see clearly. My peace and my purpose are invaluable to me. Although, I experienced and endured a lot to get where I am, this was truly worth the Golden Path that I took to get here. Even with all of these great things going well for me I recognize that when it came to bringing things into existence with the right intentions and condition, aside from what life will bring to you as you are in flow with your purpose, I left out the emotion that would be associated with whatever I was bringing into existence, the key to manifestation. This emotion is different from the barrier to The Secret Garden. This is the emotion that you feel when you are able to get your hands on that new job, house, car, your partner, your financial freedom or whatever it may be. When you leave out the emotion of what you are trying to manifest you do not allow for it to come to you as it is a moth to a flame. This was profound for me because I realized that the emotion of anything, I was trying to manifest was somewhat of an address to where I was. As I meditate and do yoga I speak my personal affirmations, visualize them and invoke the feelings of each affirmation: I am at peace at all times and it feels still, I am wise beyond my years and it feels humbling, I am healthy in all ways at all times and I feel capable, I am wealthy in all ways at all times especially financially and it feels prosperous, I am a highly effective and world renown (for the right reasons) coach, I am in flow with my life's purpose and experience overflow in God's abundance every moment of my life, and forgive me universe for my transgressions please grant me grace and mercy every moment of my life. It's always amazing that life continues to whisper to and nudge me in order to help me see, feel and know that I am close and about to experience the harvest of everything that I have sown.

Harvest of One Thousand Generations

OUTCOME

After reading this book you will see that The Golden Path that you have been on, The Secret Garden that you separated yourself in, and the process that you trusted was all worth it. As you pour out into the world, your needs are going to be met beyond what you can imagine, as you continue to perfect the proper use of what you are pouring abundance comes to you. Abundance comes when you are in flow with pouring out with the right intentions and conditions.

AUDIENCE

This is for anyone who makes statements like "I get it", "It feels good", "I can breathe", "I love where I am", "This feels right", "I have peace".

ABSTRACT

The Secret Garden has become your new reality. Your decisions or steps are in flow with what you were born to pour into the world. You realize that the circumstances you were born into and those who were before you and a part of your upbringing were necessary for you to be here. You will see how everything in your life and those around you have connected in a way that we will never understand. You will also realize that you being where you are after going through your process and using your gift has the potential to provide for generations beyond you.

QUOTE

"I looked up and realized that I took my last step, I reflected over my life and realized that the path that brought me here was worth every step of the way."

I AM STATEMENT

"I am in flow with my life's purpose and experience overflow in God's abundance every moment of my life."

FEEL IT

When you are in harvest season you feel well taken care of and you feel at ease as if there is nothing to worry about because God is taking care of everything. Without extreme effort people and circumstance will give you exactly what you need. Things will align and create joy as you recognize how things come together.

SEE IT

Can you imagine the best moment of your life? This could be graduating, the birth of a child, or marriage. Do you remember how it felt to be in that moment? Do you remember what you were thinking? The emotion of the best moment of your life is where you could be every moment of your life. This moment was not filled with what ifs or why, this moment was filled with gratitude, accomplishment, peace and joy. Imagine that the benefits, of being in flow with your purpose and pouring out your gift with the right condition and intention, could be passed down to those who come after you, your legacy. As you have poured into the world, your needs will continue to be taken care of far more than you could ever imagine. Your gift to the world will create space for you to go further and further as it is fulfilling the purpose of your life. This is what your life is meant to be, you are now reaping a Harvest of One Thousand Generations.

PRACTICE IT

Your actions should reflect that you are in The Secret Garden every moment of your life. You know what brings ease to you, you know what you have to pour into people, you know when you should pour and it feels good!

FORMULA

The Golden Path + The Secret Garden + The Seed of You + What are you Pouring + Capacity to Pour = The Harvest of One Thousand Generations (All of your needs and the needs of those who come behind you are taken care of)

ACTIVITY

Journal your entire process and see the big picture of how things connected.

FORESIGHT

2020 is the year that my cup runs over beyond what I could imagine. As I come to the end of 2019, I feel even more sure that I have gotten very close to doing everything that I was supposed to do in order to get here. Although I am not perfect as I am human and I have made a lot of "mistakes" along the way, I am grateful for where I am. My journey will always continue with the difference from then and now of me being truly alive to know how to maneuver through a situation. It's almost like a dance that you learn and over time you get better and better at it. My gift to the world is that of peace and purpose. Gifts that can change the world for the better with no monetary value. It's a gift for the inside of every person so that they can truly operate at their best within their purpose while being at peace. Everyone can reap The Harvest of One Thousand Generations if they submit to the path and process needed to get to it.